Schaum
Fingerpower
POP
LEVEL ONE

**10 PIANO SOLOS
WITH TECHNIQUE WARM-UPS**

Arranged by JAMES POTEAT

The purpose of the Fingerpower Pop series is to provide musical experiences beyond the traditional **Fingerpower**® books. The series offers students a variety of popular tunes, including hits from today's pop charts as well as classic movie themes, beloved Broadway shows, and more! The arrangements progress in order of difficulty, and many include optional accompaniments. In addition, technique warm-ups precede each pop solo.

CONTENTS

ISBN 978-1-4950-9765-2

EXCLUSIVELY DISTRIBUTED BY

HAL•LEONARD®

7777 W. BLUEMOUND RD. P.O. BOX 13819 MILWAUKEE, WI 53213

Visit Hal Leonard Online at
www.halleonard.com

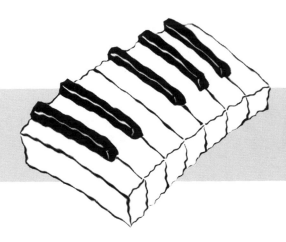

WARM-UPS

Warm-Up for
"Reindeer(s) Are Better Than People"
(page 16)

HALF-STEP/3rd PATTERN

* Repeat this warm-up starting with 3 in R.H. and 1 in L.H.

Warm-Up for
"We're Off to See the Wizard"
(page 19)

REPEATED NOTES UP THE SCALE

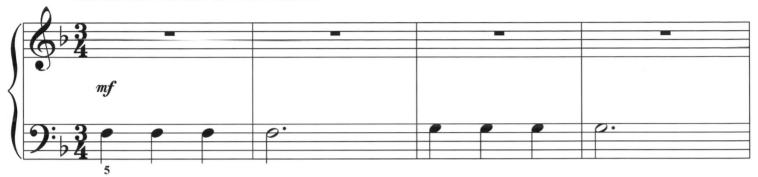

Warm-Ups for
"Let's Go Fly a Kite"
(page 22)

1. INTERVAL STUDY

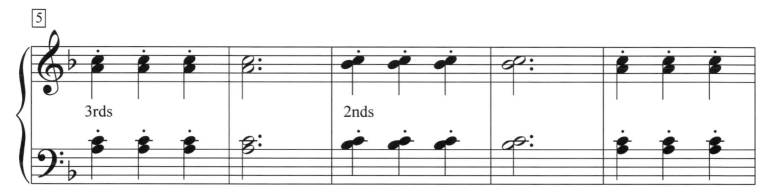

2. SHIFTING THE LEFT THUMB

Warm-Up for
"Take Me Out to the Ball Game"

(page 24)

DIFFERENT DYNAMICS

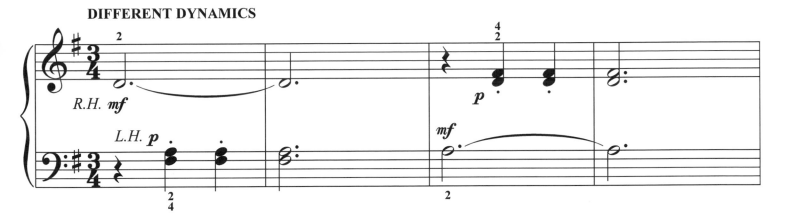

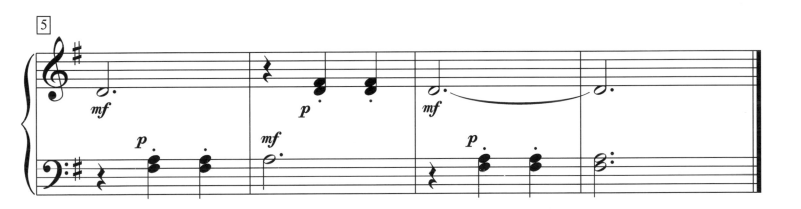

Warm-Ups for
"Somewhere Out There"
(page 26)

1. BLOCKED 3rds

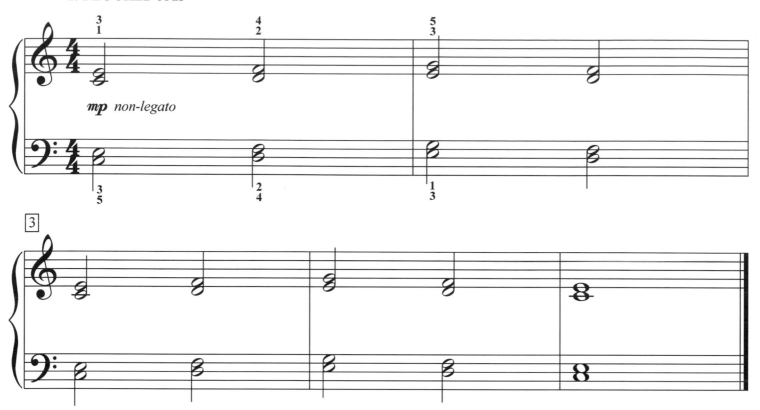

2. BROKEN 3rds

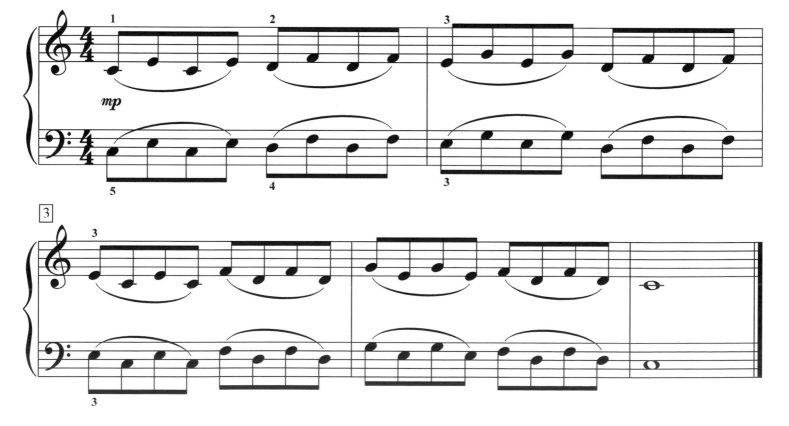

Warm-Up for
"Once Upon a Dream"

(page 28)

BLOCKED & BROKEN CHORDS

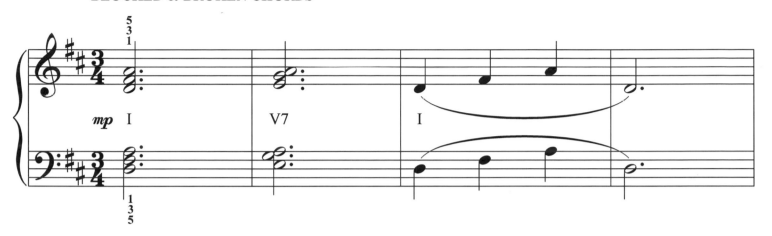

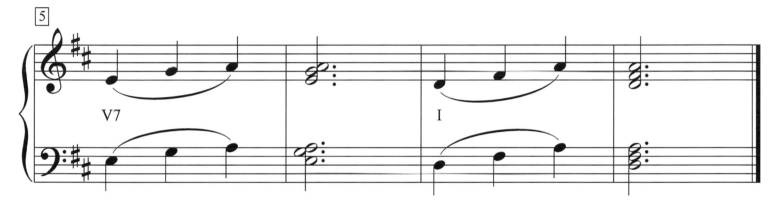

Roman Numerals & Chord Symbols

Roman numerals are used to label chords. They tell us not only the chord type (major, minor, etc.) but also which scale degree is the root of the chord. "I" means that we have a major chord based on the first note of the scale. "V7" means that we have a dominant seventh chord based on the fifth note of the scale.

Chord symbols are also used to label chords. Unlike Roman numerals, they do not tell us which scale degree is the root of the chord. "C" means that we have a major chord whose root is C. "Am" means that we have a minor chord whose root is A.

Warm-Up for
"Hallelujah"
(page 30)

BROKEN CHORDS WITH PEDAL

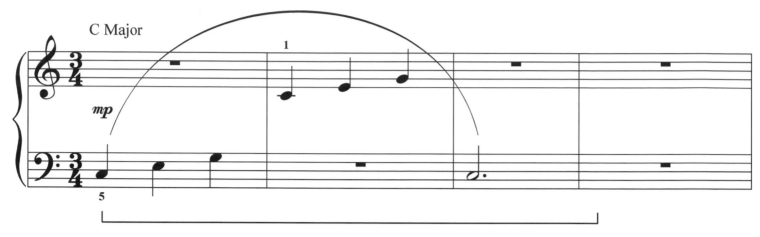

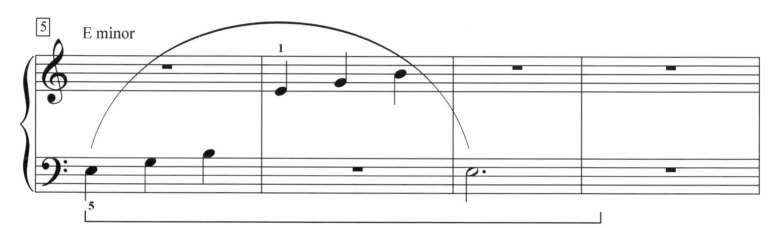

Warm-Up for
"Lean on Me"

(page 32)

BOTH HANDS LEGATO

⌊4⌋ **BOTH HANDS STACCATO**

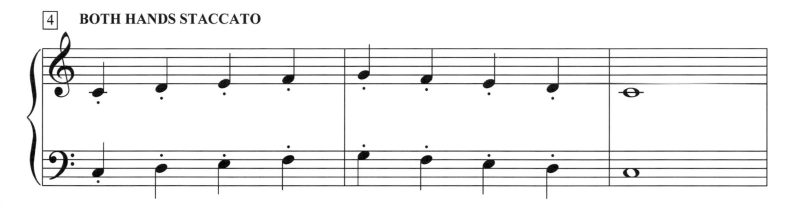

⌊7⌋ **R.H. LEGATO, L.H. STACCATO**

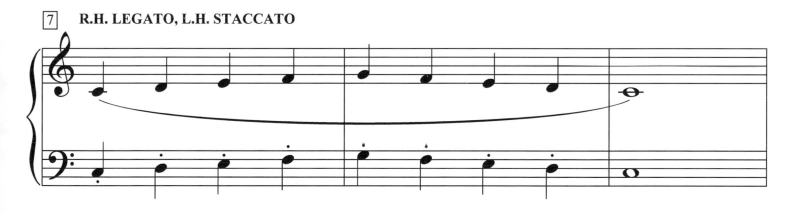

⌊10⌋ **R.H. STACCATO, L.H. LEGATO**

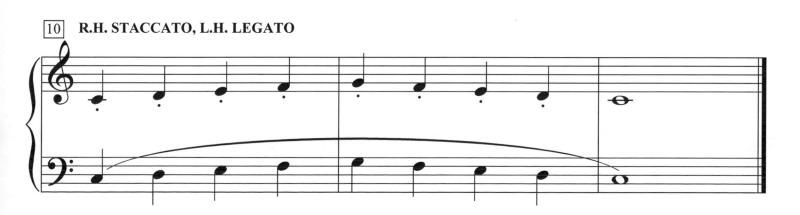

Warm-Up for "Yellow Submarine"

(page 34)

FIVE-FINGER GROUPS
Practice with straight 8ths
and swing 8ths

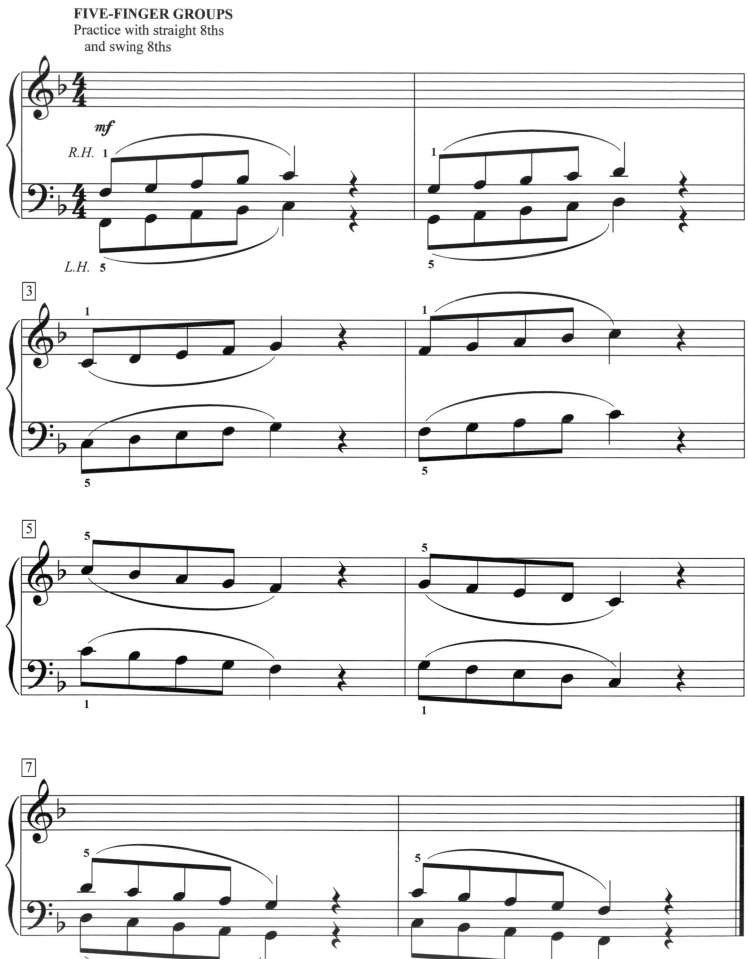

Warm-Ups for
"Shake It Off"

(page 36)

1. THREE-FINGER PHRASE

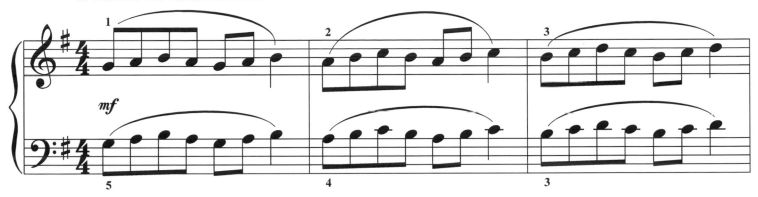

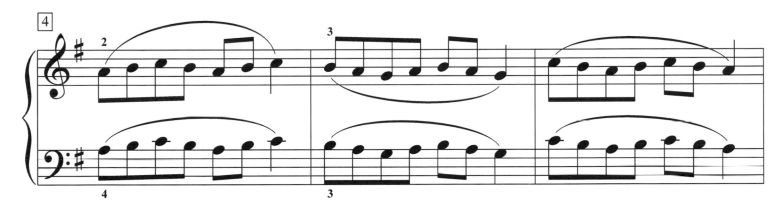

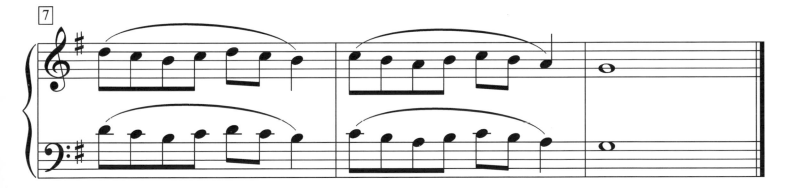

2. BLOCKED TRIADS

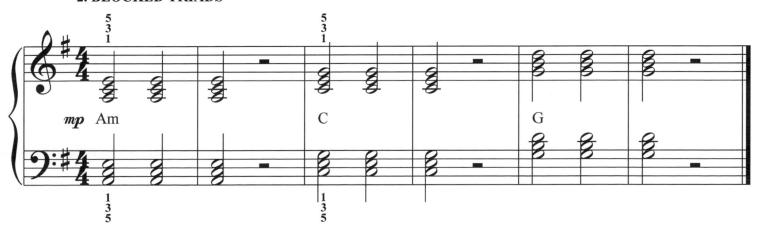

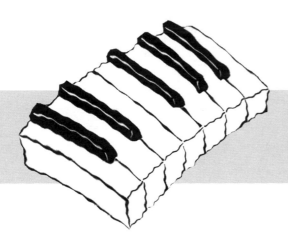

SOLOS

Reindear(s) Are Better Than People

from FROZEN

Music and Lyrics by Kristen Anderson-Lopez
and Robert Lopez
Arranged by James Poteat

WARM-UP: page 4

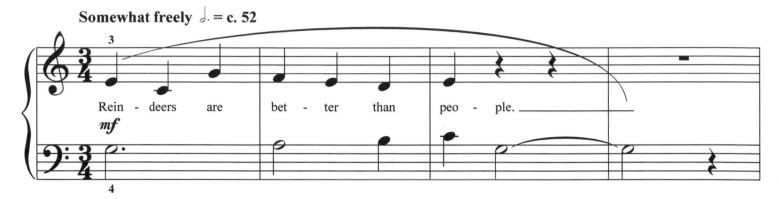

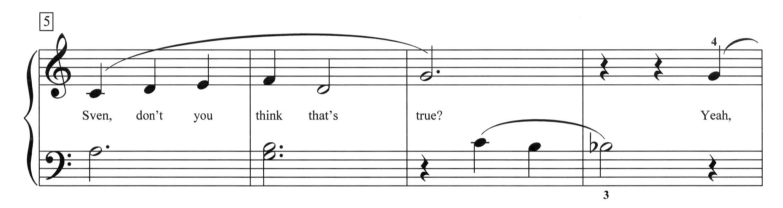

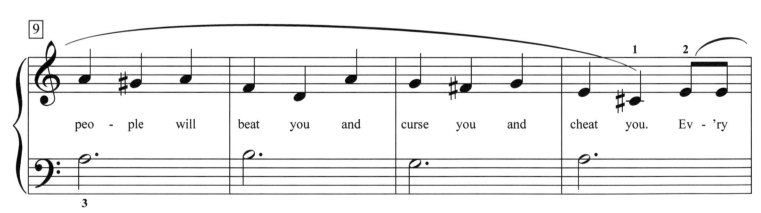

Accompaniment (Student plays one octave higher than written.)

18

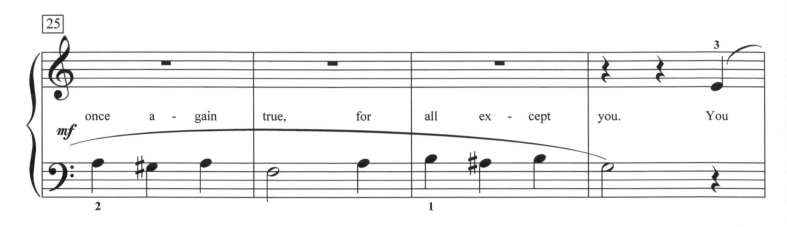

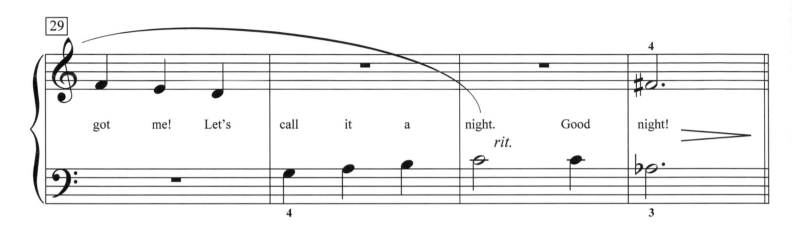

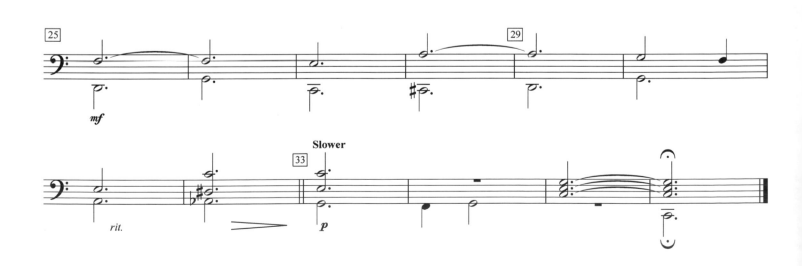

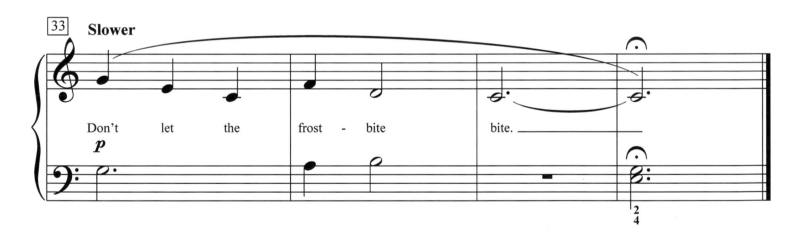

We're Off to See the Wizard

from THE WIZARD OF OZ

Lyric by E.Y. "Yip" Harburg
Music by Harold Arlen
Arranged by James Poteat

WARM-UP: page 5

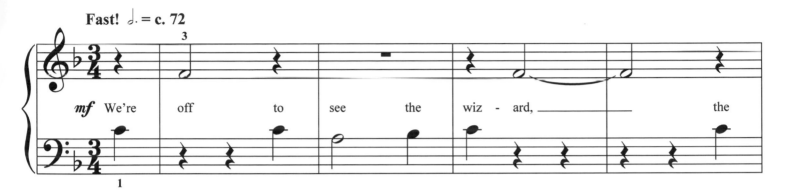

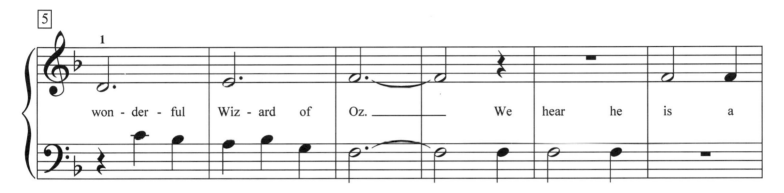

Accompaniment (Student plays one octave higher than written.)

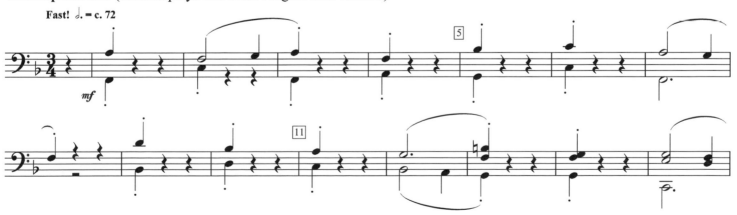

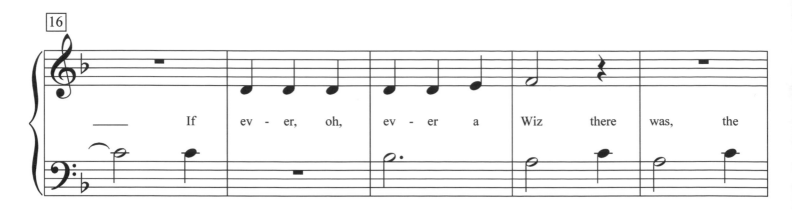

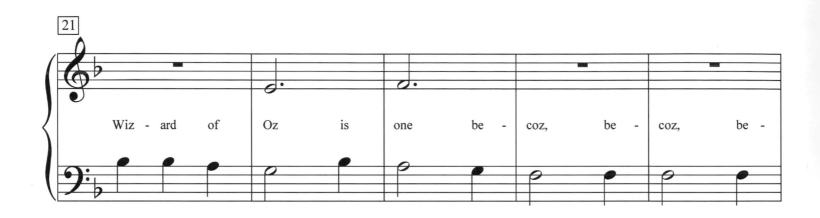

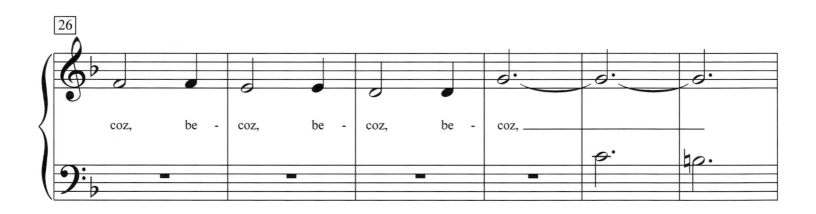

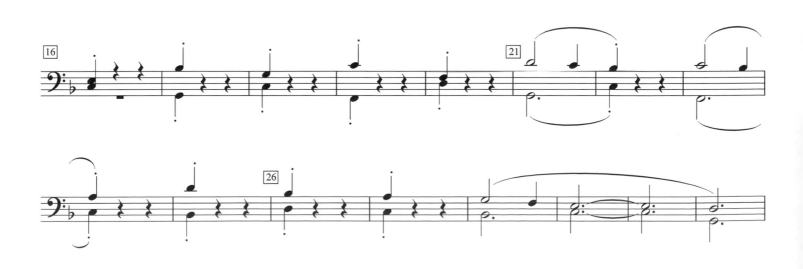

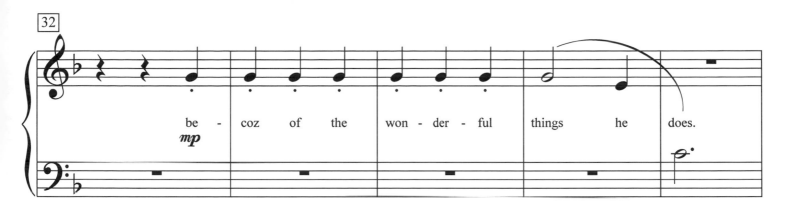

be - coz of the won - der - ful things he does.

We're off to see the

wiz - ard, _____ the won - der - ful Wiz - ard of Oz. _____

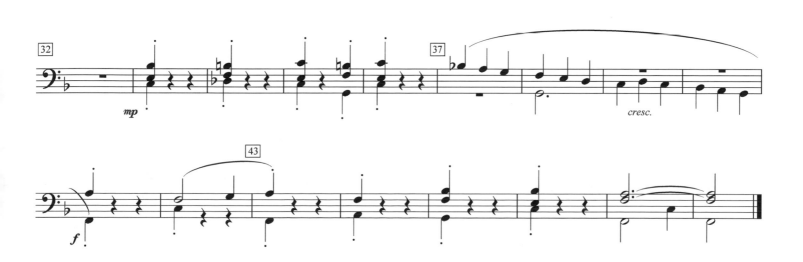

Let's Go Fly a Kite
from MARY POPPINS

Words and Music by Richard M. Sherman
and Robert B. Sherman
Arranged by James Poteat

WARM-UPS: page 6

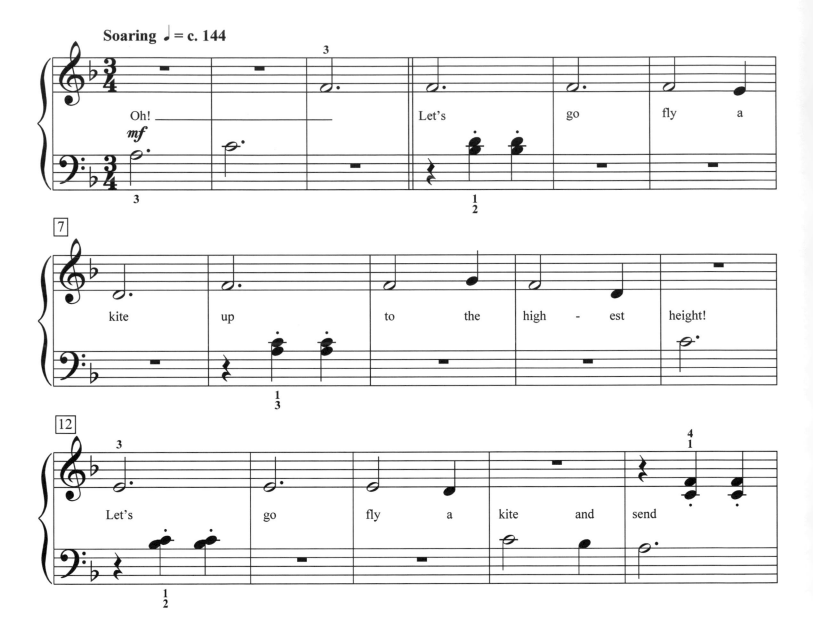

Accompaniment (Student plays one octave higher than written.)

Take Me Out to the Ball Game

Words by Jack Norworth
Music by Albert von Tilzer
Arranged by James Poteat

WARM-UP: page 7

With enthusiasm ♩ = c. 132

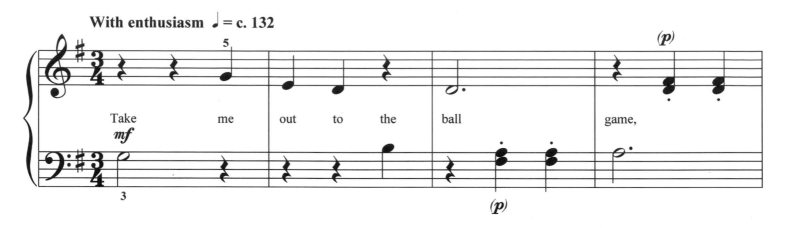

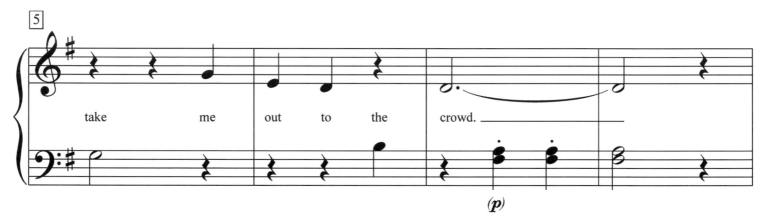

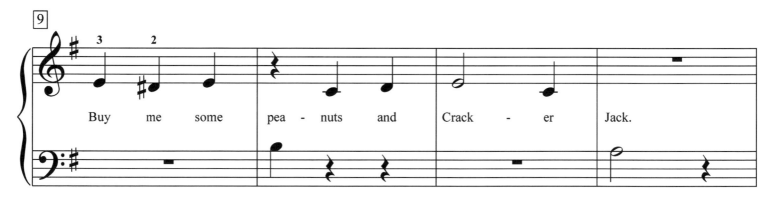

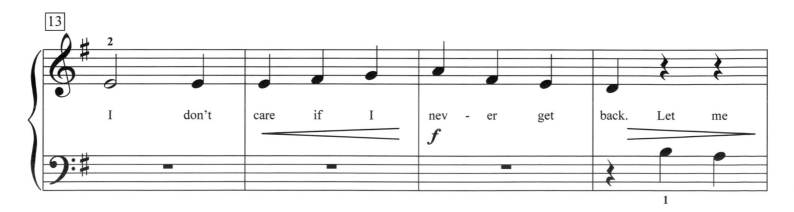

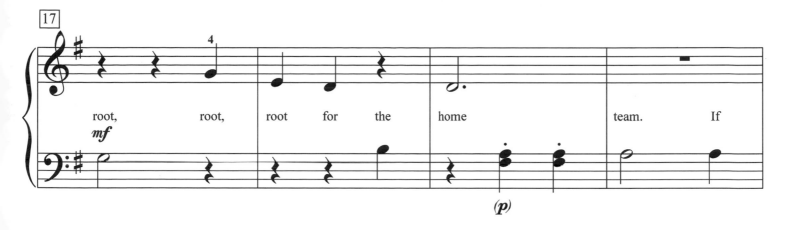

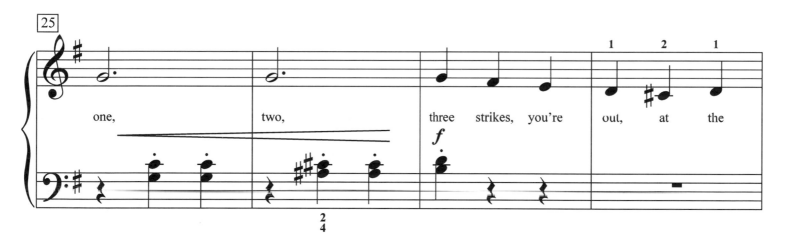

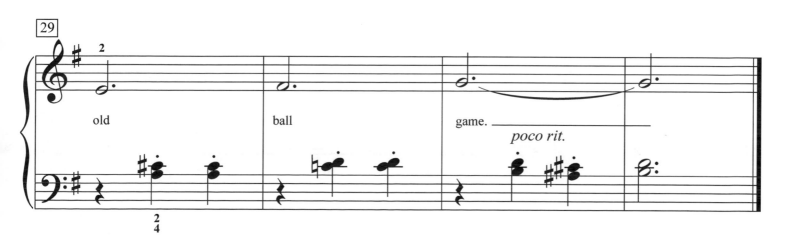

Somewhere Out There
from AN AMERICAN TAIL

Music by Barry Mann and James Horner
Lyric by Cynthia Weil

WARM-UPS: page 8

Once Upon a Dream
from SLEEPING BEAUTY

Words and Music by Sammy Fain
and Jack Lawrence
Adapted from a Theme by Tchaikovsky
Arranged by James Poteat

WARM-UP: page 9

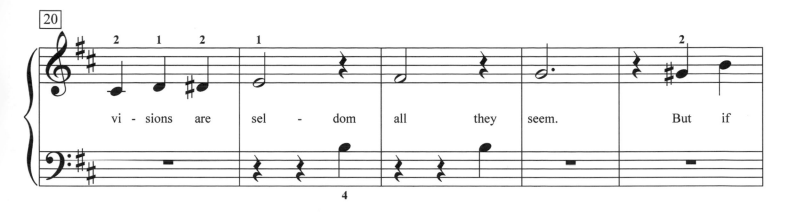

vi - sions are sel - dom all they seem. But if

I know you, I know what you'll do; you'll

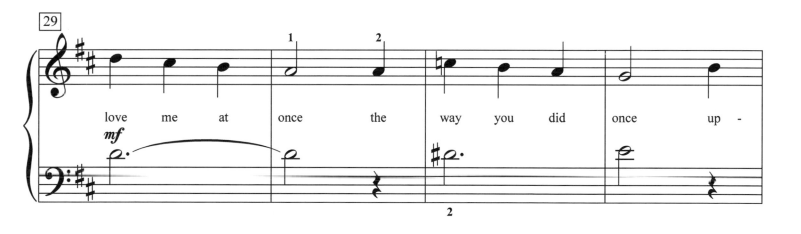

love me at once the way you did once up -

on a dream.

Hallelujah

Words and Music by
Leonard Cohen
Arranged by James Poteat

WARM-UP: page 10

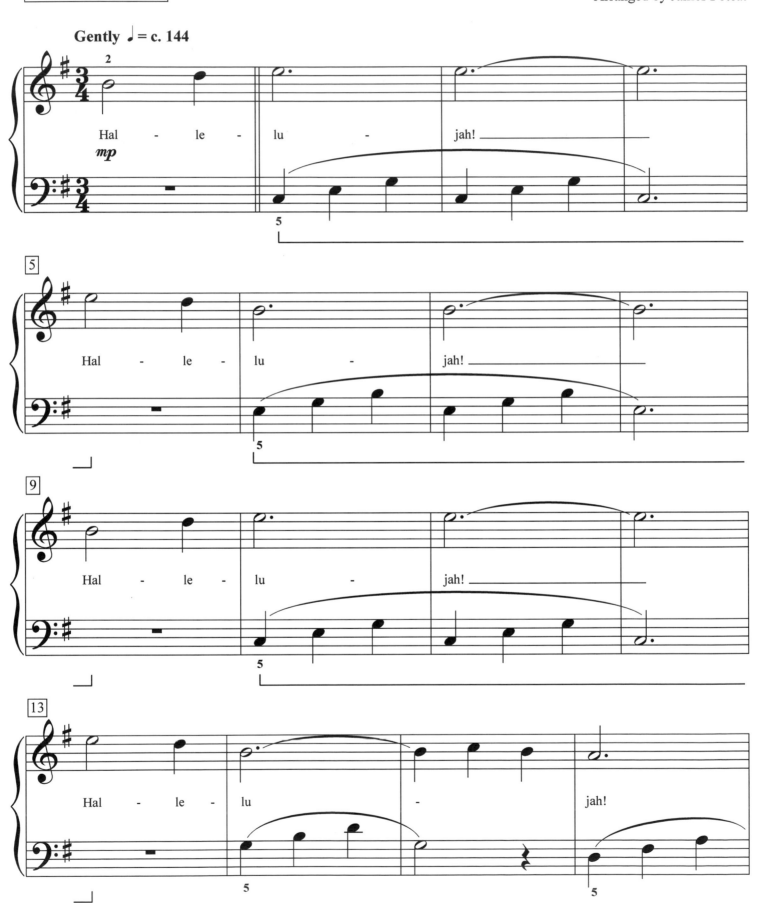

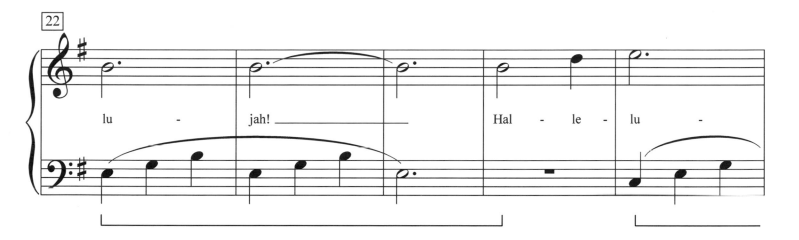

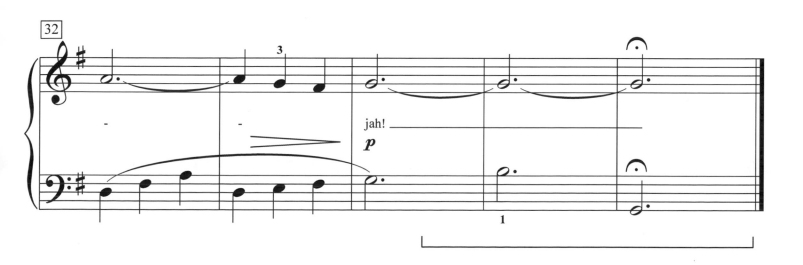

Lean on Me

Words and Music by
Bill Withers
Arranged by James Poteat

WARM-UP: page 11

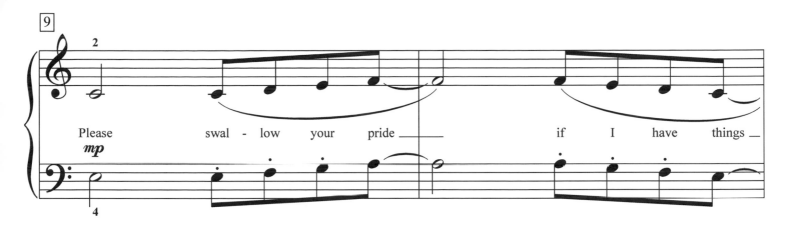

Please swal - low your pride ___ if I have things ___

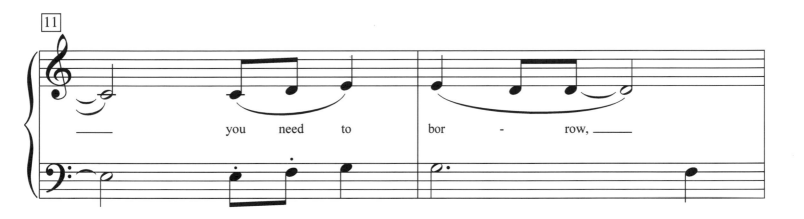

___ you need to bor - row, ___

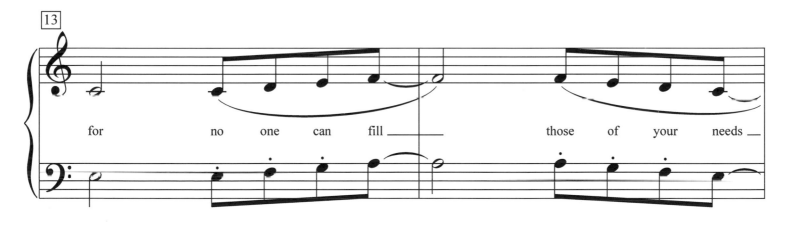

for no one can fill ___ those of your needs ___

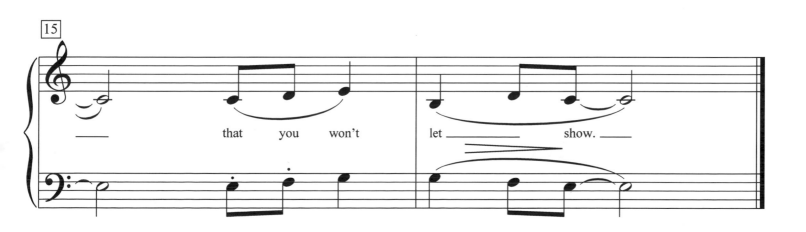

___ that you won't let ___ show. ___

Yellow Submarine

Words and Music by John Lennon
and Paul McCartney
Arranged by James Poteat

WARM-UP: page 12

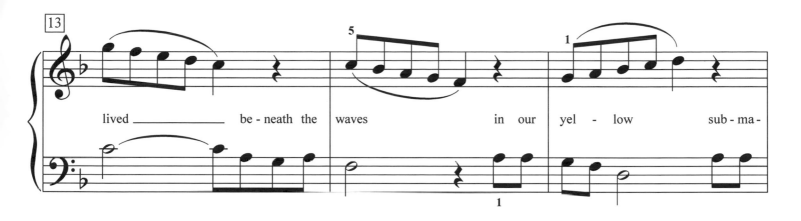

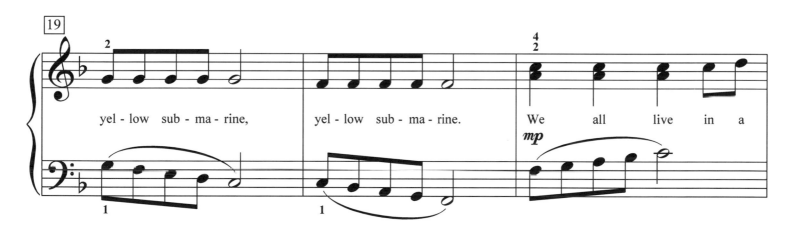

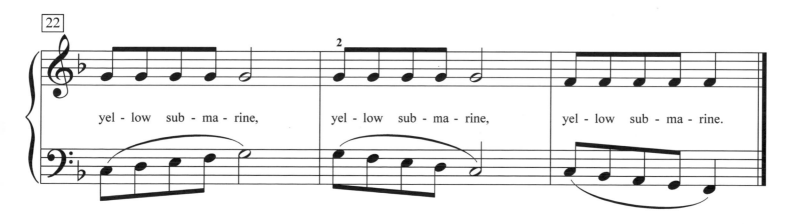

Shake It Off

Words and Music by Taylor Swift,
Max Martin and Shellback
Arranged by James Poteat

WARM-UPS: page 13

ABOUT THE ARRANGER

Since 2007 **James Poteat** has taught piano, trombone, euphonium, music theory, and composition in Woodstock, Georgia. Mr. Poteat works with students of all ages and skill levels and is equally comfortable in the worlds of popular and classical music. James is constantly arranging music for his students and is dedicated to creating and using materials of the highest quality. Learn more about James and his work by visiting **www.musicalintentions.com**.

MORE GREAT SCHAUM PUBLICATIONS

FINGERPOWER®

by John W. Schaum

Physical training and discipline are needed for both athletics and keyboard playing. Keyboard muscle conditioning is called technic. Technic exercises are as important to the keyboard player as workouts and calisthenics are to the athlete. Schaum's *Fingerpower* books are dedicated to development of individual finger strength and dexterity in both hands.

00645334 Primer Level – Book Only . . $6.95
00645016 Primer Level – Book/CD . . . $7.95
00645335 Level 1 – Book Only $6.95
00645019 Level 1 – Book/CD $7.95
00645336 Level 2 – Book Only $6.99
00645022 Level 2 – Book/CD $7.99
00645337 Level 3 – Book Only $6.95
00645025 Level 3 – Book/CD $7.99
00645338 Level 4 – Book Only $6.95
00645028 Level 4 – Book/CD $7.99
00645339 Level 5 Book Only $6.99
00645340 Level 6 Book Only $6.99

FINGERPOWER® ETUDES

Melodic exercises crafted by master technic composers. Modified or transposed etudes provide equal hand development with a planned variety of technical styles, key, and time signatures.

00645392 Primer Level $6.95
00645393 Level 1 . . . . $6.95
00645394 Level 2 . . . . $6.95
00645395 Level 3 . . . . $6.95
00645396 Level 4 . . . . $6.95

FINGERPOWER® FUN

arr. Wesley Schaum
Early Elementary Level

Musical experiences beyond the traditional *Fingerpower* books that include fun to play pieces with finger exercises and duet accompaniments. Short technic prepatory drills (finger workouts) focus on melodic patterns found in each piece.

00645126 Primer Level $6.95
00645127 Level 1 . . . . $6.95
00645128 Level 2 . . . . $6.95
00645129 Level 3 . . . . $6.95
00645144 Level 4 . . . . $6.95

FINGERPOWER® TRANSPOSER

by Wesley Schaum
Early Elementary Level

This book includes 21 short, 8-measure exercises using 5-finger patterns. Positions are based on C,F, and G major and no key signatures are used. Patterns involve intervals of 3rds, 4ths, and 5ths up and down and are transposed from C to F and F to C, C to G and G to C, G to F and F to G.

00645150 Primer Level $6.95
00645151 Level 1 . . . . $6.95
00645152 Level 2 . . . . $6.95
00645154 Level 3 . . . . $6.95
00645156 Level 4 . . . . $6.95

JUMBO STAFF MANUSCRIPT BOOK

This pad features 24 pages with 4 staves per page.
00645936 . . . . $4.25

CERTIFICATE OF MUSICAL ACHIEVEMENT

Reward your students for their hard work with these official 8x10 inch certificates that you can customize. 12 per package.
00645938 . . . . $5.99

SCHAUM LESSON ASSIGNMENT BOOK

by John Schaum

With space for 32 weeks, this book will help keep students on the right track for their practice time.
00645935 . . . . $3.95

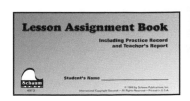

Prices, contents,
and availability subject
to change without notice.